skewered

skewered

cooking food on sticks, picks, spikes and spears

Susannah Blake

LORENZ BOOKS

This edition is published by Lorenz Books

Lorenz Books is an imprint of Anness Publishing Ltd
Hermes House, 88–89 Blackfriars Road, London SE1 8HA
tel. 020 7401 2077; fax 020 7633 9499
www.lorenzbooks.com; info@anness.com

This edition distributed in the UK by The Manning Partnership Ltd, 6 The Old Dairy
Melcombe Road, Bath BA2 3LR; tel. 01225 478 444; fax 01225 478 440
sales@manning-partnership.co.uk

This edition distributed in the USA and Canada by National Book Network
4501 Forbes Boulevard, Suite 200, Lanham, MD 20706; tel. 301 459 3366
fax 301 429 5746; www.nbnbooks.com

This edition distributed in Australia by Pan Macmillan Australia, Level 18, St Martins
Tower, 31 Market St, Sydney, NSW 2000; tel. 1300 135 113; fax 1300 135 103
customer.service@macmillan.com.au

This edition distributed in New Zealand by David Bateman Ltd, 30 Tarndale Grove
Off Bush Road, Albany, Auckland; tel. (09) 415 7664; fax (09) 415 8892

A CIP catalogue record for this book is available from the British Library.

Publisher: Joanna Lorenz
Managing Editor: Linda Fraser
Senior Editor: Susannah Blake
Editorial Reader: Marija Duric Speare
Photographers: Frank Adam, Tim Auty, Martin Brigdale, Nicki Dowey
Recipes by: Kit Chan, Yasuko Fukuoko, Becky Johnson, Maggie Mayhew, Sallie Morris,
Rena Salaman, Marlena Spieler, Linda Tubby, Sunil Vijayakar and Kate Whitman
Designer: Mark Latter
Production Controller: Pedro Nelson

10 9 8 7 6 5 4 3 2 1

NOTES
Bracketed terms are intended for American readers.

For all recipes, quantities are given in both metric and imperial measures and, where
appropriate, measures are also given in standard cups and spoons. Follow one set, but
not a mixture, because they are not interchangeable.

Standard spoon and cup measures are level.
1 tsp = 5ml, 1 tbsp = 15ml, 1 cup = 250ml/8fl oz

Australian standard tablespoons are 20ml. Australian readers should use 3 tsp in place
of 1 tbsp for measuring small quantities of gelatine, flour, salt, etc.

Medium (US large) eggs are used unless otherwise stated.

contents

Skewering

This book celebrates and extols the versatility and ease of cooking with the humble skewer and offers some surprising and tantalizing recipes. Fresh ingredients from around the world are spiked or speared and transformed into exciting meals and tempting snacks for every occasion.

Skewers come in all shape and sizes. The French call them *brochettes*, Russians call them *shashlik*, Italians call them *spendini* and the Turks call them *kebabs*. The variety and appeal of skewers, whether they are the sword-like, steel variety, matchstick-thin bamboo spikes, intricately carved Japanese pick-sticks or fragrant herb stems, make selecting a skewer almost as exciting as deciding what kinds of foods to spear on them.

A vast array of foods can be speared, marinated and stored in the refrigerator ready for a quick grilling for a barbecue or a party. Whether it's tiny spiced balls of tender chicken or little shallots, hunks of firm fresh fish or cubes of tasty soft cheese, they all lend themselves perfectly to skewering.

As well as a whole variety of foods to skewer, many recipes include delicious sweet and savoury sauces that are just perfect for dipping skewered bites into, plus there are fabulous ideas for making intensely flavoured marinades and spice rubs to really tantalize the tastebuds.

TYPES OF SKEWER

Skewers come in many different shapes and sizes and may be made of metal, wood or even woody herb stems. They can range from the simplest bamboo skewers to pretty metal skewers with intricately decorated handles.

Metal Skewers

Traditionally, in the West, skewers were made of metal. Look for flattened skewers rather than round ones; the food is less likely to roll when you turn them. Double pronged skewers help to keep the ingredients from slipping or sliding off. It is wise to buy stainless steel skewers to avoid tainting food with a metallic taste.

Bamboo Skewers

These classic Asian-style skewers come in several different lengths and are widely available. They are very cheap and are thrown away after one use. Be sure to soak them for at least 20 minutes before threading them to ensure that they do not burn during cooking.

Always soak bamboo skewers in water before use to prevent them burning.

Simple metal skewers are perfect for threading tougher ingredients such as cubes of meat.

Fragrant Skewers

Herbs with woody stems such as rosemary, or hard aromatic stems such as lemon grass make perfect skewers. They can impart a wonderful flavour and look very pretty. To use herbs, strip away the bottom leaves with your fingers and use the stripped end to spear the food. Softer foods such as tofu or prawns (shrimp) will thread straight on but tougher meats or vegetables will need to be speared with a metal skewer first. To make lemon grass skewers, strip away any brown outer leaves, then slice diagonally across one end to make a sharp point and use to spear food.

CHOOSING FOODS TO SKEWER

A wide variety of foods can be cooked on skewers. Combine ingredients that complement each other in flavour, colour and shape.

Meat, Poultry and Game

Beef, pork, lamb and chicken are classic ingredients for kebabs and go well with Mediterranean vegetables. Choose tender cuts that cook quickly. Leave some of the fat on the meat, add strips of streaky (fatty) bacon or marinade and baste with oils to keep the meat moist. If using chicken, use tender breast fillets. Game such as pheasant, duck or partridge can also be skewered. Marinate with warm spices and skewer with slices of orange or apple and mushrooms.

Skewer simple strips of chicken, then grill them and serve with a spicy dip and fresh salad.

Cubes of ice cream can be pushed on to skewers to make a summer dessert.

Small soft fruits such as strawberries and plums are perfect for skewering.

Fish and Shellfish

Healthy and quick to cook, these are great on skewers. Choose firm fish such as salmon, cod and monkfish. Prawns (shrimp) are perfect for skewering too. Try oysters with spicy sausage, or scallops with bacon and asparagus.

Vegetarian Ingredients

There is a huge choice for vegetarians, from cubes of tofu and chunks of vegetarian sausage to vegetables, fruits and cheeses. Slow-cooking vegetables such as pumpkin or new potatoes can also be skewered and grilled, but should be par-boiled first.

Sweet Foods

You can make fabulous desserts by skewering sweet foods such as fruit, marshmallows and cubes of ice cream. Sweet skewers are great served with a delicious dipping sauce or a creamy fondue.

PREPARATION AND COOKING

Food for skewering should be trimmed of any inedible parts and cut into bitesize pieces. When combining different ingredients on one skewer, ensure that each piece of food requires the same cooking time. For example, peppers cook quickly so cut slower cooking ingredients small so that they all finish cooking at the same time. Quick-cooking ingredients, such as cherry tomatoes, could be added to the skewer halfway through cooking or threaded on to separate skewers.

Threading Food
Don't overload skewers; always allow a little space between pieces so that each one is exposed to the same amount of heat. If cooking something wide and flat such as butterflied prawns (shrimp) consider using two skewers so that the food remains flat.

Always thread the skewer through the centre of each piece of food.

Baste food during cooking to keep it moist and help it brown evenly.

BASIC COOKING TIMES
Chicken cubes (2.5cm/1in): about 5 minutes each side; test that meat is opaque and juices run clear when pierced with the point of a knife.
Chicken strips: 2–4 minutes each side until cooked through.
Pork cubes (2.5cm/1in): 6–8 minutes each side; check that meat is cooked through (it should no longer be pink in the middle).
Fish cubes (2.5cm/1in): 2–4 minutes each side until the flesh is opaque and flakes easily.
Lamb cubes (2.5cm/1in): about 5 minutes each side; the flesh can remain pink in the centre but check it is hot all the way through.
Beef cubes (2.5cm/1in): 4–6 minutes each side; steak can remain pink in the centre but check it is hot all the way through.

Marinating and Basting
You can add flavour to food and also tenderize meat by marinating it before cooking. During cooking baste the food with the marinade or oil to keep it moist and help it brown evenly. If using sweet sauces or marinades, only brush on a few minutes before the end of cooking time to prevent the sugar from burning.

Cooking Skewers
Skewers are usually cooked under a grill (broiler), on a ridged griddle pan or on a barbecue, which will add an intense, smoky flavour. Cook skewers over a medium to medium-low temperature and keep the handles away from the heat. (Metal skewers conduct heat through their whole length so always use an oven glove when turning or lifting them.)

MAKING MARINADES

All kinds of foods benefit from being marinated before cooking. Marinades add flavour and are also used to tenderize and add moisture to raw meat, poultry and fish.

Most marinades include an oil mixed with an acid such as vinegar or lemon juice. Other flavourings may be added to this basic mix. Liquid flavourings include wine, sherry, yogurt, coconut milk and fruit juices, while a variety of herbs, spices and other seasonings are good dry flavourings.

Marinating times will vary depending on the food being marinated. Ten minutes will make a difference but the longer the time the more intense the results.

Mediterranean Garlic Marinade

Ideal for both marinating and basting meat, fish or vegetables.

Makes about 450ml/¾ pint/scant 2 cups

300ml/½ pint/1¼ cups white wine
150ml/¼ pint/⅔ cup olive oil
3 garlic cloves, crushed
small bunch chopped parsley or oregano
   or basil (optional)
salt and ground black pepper

Whisk together all the ingredients, then marinate the food for at least 30 minutes, turning occasionally.

Chinese-style Marinade

A sweet and sour combination for seafood, chicken and vegetables.

Makes about 450ml/¾ pint/scant 2 cups

45ml/3 tbsp lemon or lime juice
45ml/3 tbsp rice or white wine vinegar
30ml/2 tbsp soy sauce
15ml/1 tbsp dry sherry or sake
15ml/1 tbsp sesame oil
60ml/4 tbsp groundnut (peanut) oil
15ml/1 tbsp light brown sugar
2.5ml/½ tsp Chinese five-spice powder
small bunch coriander (cilantro), chopped
salt and ground black pepper

Whisk together the citrus juice, vinegar, soy sauce, sherry and sesame oil, then gradually whisk in the groundnut oil. Stir in the remaining ingredients and marinate the food for at least 2 hours.

Thai-style Marinade

This aromatic and spicy marinade will be perfect with fish and shellfish, chicken, beef or pork.

Makes about 450ml/¾ pint/scant 2 cups

75ml/5 tbsp lime juice
45ml/3 tbsp fish sauce or soy sauce
150ml/¼ pint/⅔ cup coconut milk
2 garlic cloves, crushed
25ml/1½ tbsp light brown sugar
5ml/1 tsp Thai red curry paste or
   1 lemon grass stalk, finely chopped
   and 1.25ml/¼ tsp dried chilli flakes
small bunch coriander (cilantro), chopped
sea salt and ground black pepper

Combine the lime juice with the fish or soy sauce, then whisk in the coconut milk. Stir in the remaining ingredients and marinate the food for at least 2 hours.

Sweet Marinade

A spiced mixture that goes well with beef and lamb, but is also ideal for duck, chicken and fish.

Makes about 150ml/¼ pint/⅔ cup
75g/3oz/6 tbsp butter, melted
30ml/2 tbsp brandy or kirsch or marsala
grated rind and juice of 1 orange
10ml/2 tsp ground cinnamon
2.5cm/1in piece fresh root ginger, finely
    grated or 10ml/2 tsp ground ginger
30ml/2 tbsp clear honey
pinch of freshly grated nutmeg

Whisk the ingredients together, then leave the food to marinate for at least 30 minutes. Sweet marinades tend to burn. To prevent this, only brush the marinade on a few minutes before the end of the cooking time.

USING SPICES AND AROMATICS

Another way of adding flavour is to rub the meat or fish with dry ground spices or a moist curry paste. This works particularly well if a crisp exterior is required. Electric spice grinders can make quick work of grinding whole spices, but you can also use a mortar and pestle. Choose an Asian-style mortar that has a rough surface because this will grip the spices and prevent them flying out as you pound them.

Cajun Rub

This is a particularly good recipe for spare ribs, chicken and beef.

Makes about 100g/3½oz/1 cup
2 garlic cloves, crushed
1–2 small red chillies, finely chopped (seeds
    removed if you prefer a milder blend)
5ml/1 tsp ground coriander seeds
10ml/2 tsp ground cumin seeds
5ml/1 tsp fennel seeds
5ml/1 tsp ground cardamom seeds
leaves from a small bunch each of sage,
    oregano and thyme, finely chopped
15ml/1 tbsp light brown sugar
salt and ground black pepper

Blend or grind all the ingredients together then rub over the meat. Leave to marinate for at least 3 hours before cooking.

Rosemary Rub

This goes remarkably well with chicken, lamb, pork and beef.

Makes about 75ml/5 tbsp
60ml/4 tbsp chopped fresh rosemary
2 garlic cloves, crushed
5ml/1 tsp mustard powder
5ml/1 tsp dried oregano or mixed herbs
salt and ground black pepper

Grind all the ingredients together to form a coarse powder. Rub over the meat and leave to stand for 2 hours.

Fresh Herbs

Herb leaves can be skewered along with other ingredients to add flavour. Try chicken cubes interspersed with bay leaves, chunks of fish with fennel fronds, or rosemary sticks threaded with lamb.

snacks on sticks

Delicious morsels spiked on little sticks or decorative skewers make perfect bites to serve with pre-dinner drinks. They're also great for munching on when you need a little something to keep your appetite at bay. Offer guests fabulous delights such as grilled chicken balls on bamboo skewers or spiked seafood.

These Japanese-inspired skewers are made with tofu, aubergine and konnyaku. Konnyaku is a mildly flavoured, gelatinous cake made from the konnyaku plant. It can be found in Japanese food stores.

grilled vegetable sticks

Serves 4

INGREDIENTS
275g/10oz tofu
250g/9oz konnyaku
2 small aubergines (eggplant)
25ml/1½ tbsp toasted sesame oil

**For the yellow
and green sauces**
45ml/3 tbsp shiro miso (yellow
   soybean paste)
15ml/1 tbsp caster (superfine) sugar
5 young spinach leaves
salt
2.5ml/½ tsp sansho (Japanese pepper)

For the red sauce
15ml/1 tbsp miso (soybean paste)
5ml/1 tsp caster (superfine) sugar
5ml/1 tsp mirin (sweet rice wine)

To garnish
large pinch of white poppy seeds
15ml/1 tbsp toasted sesame seeds

1 Wrap the tofu in three layers of kitchen paper. Set a chopping board on top to press out any liquid. Leave for 30 minutes, then cut into eight 7.5 x 2 x 1cm/3 x ¾ x ½ in slices.

2 Drain the konnyaku, cut it in half and put in a pan with enough water to cover. Bring to the boil and cook for 5 minutes. Drain and cut it into eight slices. Slice the aubergines lengthways into four flat slices. Soak in water for 15 minutes. Drain and pat dry.

3 Make the yellow sauce. Combine the miso and sugar in a pan and cook over a low heat, stirring until the sugar has dissolved. Pour half the sauce into a small bowl. Blanch the spinach for 30 seconds and drain, then cool under running water. Squeeze out the water and chop finely. Transfer to a mortar and pound to a paste using a pestle. Add the paste and sansho to the yellow sauce in the pan and mix to make the green sauce.

4 Make the red sauce. Put the miso, sugar and mirin in a small pan and cook over a low heat, stirring until the sugar has dissolved. Remove from the heat. Preheat the grill.

5 Pierce the tofu, konnyaku and aubergine pieces with two bamboo skewers each. Brush the aubergine with sesame oil and grill (broil) for 15 minutes, turning several times. Grill the konnyaku and tofu slices for 3–5 minutes each side. Remove but keep the grill hot.

6 Spread the red miso sauce on the aubergine slices. Spread one side of the tofu slices with green sauce and one side of the konnyaku with the yellow sauce. Grill for 1–2 minutes. Sprinkle with poppy and sesame seeds, and serve.

Hard salty cheese cubes spiked with bay leaves and drenched in tangy lemon juice make perfect pre-dinner snacks for a crowd or finger food at parties. They take only minutes to cook and are delicious with a really cold resinous wine, plenty of excellent olives, fruity olive oil and rustic, crusty bread for dipping.

kefalotyri cubes spiked with bay leaves

Serves 6

INGREDIENTS
18 large bay leaves or mixed bay and lemon leaves
275g/10oz Kefalotyri cheese, cut into 18 cubes
20ml/4 tsp extra virgin olive oil
ground black pepper

1 Soak 18 bamboo skewers in water for 20 minutes. Add the bay and/or lemon leaves to prevent them from burning during cooking.

2 Put the cheese cubes in a dish large enough to hold the skewers. Pour over the olive oil. Sprinkle over a little pepper and toss. Drain the skewers, then thread them with the cheese and drained bay leaves and/or lemon leaves. Put the skewers of cheese back in the oil.

3 Prepare and light the barbecue. Place the skewers on the barbecue, spacing them evenly and ensuring they are not too close to the heat. Grill for about 5 seconds on each side. The pieces of cheese should have golden-brown lines, and should be just starting to melt. Serve immediately.

crispy coconut prawns

These tasty golden morsels are great pop-in-the-mouth snacks and make a perfect hors d'oeuvre to serve with drinks. The delicate flavour of prawn in a light coconut coating contrasts perfectly with the rich, spicy peanut dipping sauce.

Serves 6–8

INGREDIENTS
115g/4oz/1 cup plain
  (all-purpose) flour
5ml/1 tsp baking powder
5ml/1 tsp mild curry powder
2.5ml/½ tsp paprika
5ml/1 tsp sea salt
275ml/9fl oz/generous 1 cup beer
2 large (US extra large) eggs,
  lightly beaten
200g/7oz/2½ cups desiccated (dry
  unsweetened shredded) coconut
24 raw tiger prawns (jumbo shrimp),
  peeled and tails intact
sunflower oil, for deep-frying

For the dipping sauce
15ml/1 tbsp smooth peanut butter
15ml/1 tbsp dark soy sauce
45ml/3 tbsp sweet chilli sauce
45ml/3 tbsp crème fraîche
1 garlic clove, finely minced (ground)
  or crushed
finely grated rind of 1 lime
juice of 2 large limes

1 Mix together all the ingredients for the sauce in a bowl and set aside. In a separate bowl, combine the flour, baking and curry powder, paprika and salt. Add the beer and the eggs, then stir until just combined. Fold in 25g/1oz/⅓ cup of the coconut.

2 Thread each prawn lengthways, from head to tail, on to a bamboo skewer and spread the remaining coconut in a deep soup plate or a shallow bowl. Pour the sunflower oil into a deep wok to a depth of 7.5cm/3in and heat to 190°C/375°F.

3 Working in batches, dip the skewered prawns into the batter (letting the excess batter drip back into the bowl), then lightly roll them in the coconut to coat.

4 Deep-fry the prawns, in batches, for 2–3 minutes, or until golden. Drain on a wire rack placed over crumpled kitchen paper and serve with the sauce.

Don't overmix
When making the beer batter, be careful to stir it only very briefly. Overmixing will spoil the light and delicate texture.

Serves 12

INGREDIENTS
a piece of sugar cane
   cut into 12 spikes or
   12 bamboo skewers
400g/14oz
   Mediterranean
   prawns (jumbo
   shrimp), peeled
225g/8oz skinned
   cod or halibut
   fillet, roughly
   cut into pieces
pinch of ground
   turmeric
1.5ml/¼ tsp ground
   white pepper
1.5ml/¼ tsp salt
60ml/4 tbsp chopped
   fresh coriander
   (cilantro)
1 fresh long red chilli,
   seeded and finely
   chopped
30ml/2 tbsp
   sunflower oil

For the tolee molee
25g/1oz/½ cup
   coriander leaves
45ml/3 tbsp olive oil
300g/11oz sweet
   onions, halved and
   finely sliced
90ml/6 tbsp
   balachaung (chilli
   and prawn paste)
15ml/1 tbsp sugar
juice of ½ lime
30ml/2 tbsp water

These little bites are inspired by Burmese tolee molee (bits and pieces that accompany a main course). The dips and skewers are easy to prepare yet they are full of flavour and make ideal snacks. In the summer, they are great cooked over a barbecue.

seafood spiked on sugar cane with tolee molee

1 Soak the sugar cane spikes or bamboo skewers in water for 30 minutes. Meanwhile, using a small knife, make a shallow cut down the centre of the curved back of the prawns. Pull out the black vein with the point of the knife.

2 Slice the prawns roughly and place in a food processor with the fish, turmeric, pepper and salt. Pulse until the mixture forms a paste. Add the coriander and chilli and pulse lightly to combine with the other ingredients. Spoon into a bowl and chill for 30 minutes.

3 Make the tolee molee. Put the coriander leaves in cold water and chill. Heat the oil in a large frying pan, then add the onion and fry for 10 minutes, stirring occasionally. Increase the heat until the onions are golden and crisp. Pile them into a serving bowl.

4 Place the balachaung in a serving bowl. Put the sugar, lime juice and water in a small jug (pitcher) and mix together, then stir into the balachaung and set aside.

5 Using damp hands, mould the seafood mixture around the drained sugar cane spikes, or bamboo skewers, to form oval, sausage shapes.

6 Preheat the grill (broiler) and brush the seafood with the sunflower oil. Grill (broil) for about 3 minutes each side until just cooked through. Serve immediately with the tolee molee.

Chopping sugar cane
Sugar cane is widely available from ethnic food stores. To make the spikes, chop through the length of the sugar cane using a cleaver or heavy cook's knife and split into 1cm/½in shards.

In Japan, these little chicken balls are a yakitori bar favourite but they also make a great family dish. They can be eaten straight from the stick and are especially popular with children.

grilled chicken balls with yakitori sauce

Serves 4

INGREDIENTS

300g/11oz skinless chicken, minced (ground)
2 eggs
2.5ml/½ tsp salt
10ml/2 tsp plain (all-purpose) flour
10ml/2 tsp cornflour (cornstarch)
90ml/6 tbsp dried breadcrumbs
2.5cm/1in piece fresh root ginger, grated
shichimi togarashi (seven-spice powder) or sansho (Japanese pepper), to garnish

For the yakitori sauce

60ml/4 tbsp sake
75ml/5 tbsp shoyu (Japanese soy sauce)
15ml/1 tbsp mirin (sweet rice wine)
15ml/1 tbsp caster (superfine) sugar
2.5ml/½ tsp cornflour (cornstarch) blended with 5ml/1 tsp water

1 Soak eight bamboo skewers in water overnight. Put all the ingredients for the chicken balls, except the ginger, in a food processor and blend well. Wet your hands and scoop about a tablespoonful of the mixture into your palm. Shape it into a small ball about half the size of a golf ball. Make a further 30–32 balls in the same way.

2 Squeeze the juice from the grated ginger into a small mixing bowl. Discard the pulp, then add the ginger juice to a small pan of boiling water. Add the chicken balls, and boil for about 7 minutes, or until the colour of the meat changes and the balls float to the surface. Remove and drain on kitchen paper.

3 In a small pan, mix all the ingredients for the yakitori sauce, except for the cornflour liquid. Bring to the boil, then reduce the heat and simmer for about 10 minutes. Add the cornflour liquid and stir until thick. Transfer to a bowl.

4 Thread three or four balls on to each skewer. Cook under a medium grill (broiler) or on a barbecue, keeping the skewer handles away from the fire. Turn them frequently for a few minutes, or until the balls start to brown. Brush with sauce and return to the heat. Repeat the process twice. Serve, sprinkled with shichimi togarashi or sansho.

small and spiked

Skewered bites make a great appetizer or a fabulous light meal when served with an accompaniment. Delicious nibbles such as honey-glazed chicken satay or griddled pork on lemon grass sticks make tasty appetizers. Or team grilled swordfish skewers or spiked sardine parcels with a large salad for a light lunch or supper.

These tasty skewers look really pretty and make a great light lunch or supper served with salad. Give each guest an individual dish of dip so that they can dunk to their heart's content.

potato and shallot skewers with grainy mustard dip

1 Prepare a barbecue or preheat the grill (broiler). Make the dip. Place the garlic, egg yolks and lemon juice in a food processor or blender and process the ingredients for a few seconds until smooth.

2 Keep the motor running and add the oil gradually, pouring it in a thin stream, until the mixture forms a thick, glossy cream. Stir in the mustard and season with salt and pepper. Chill until ready to use.

3 Par-boil the potatoes in boiling water for about 5 minutes. Drain well, then thread potatoes on to short skewers, alternating them with the shallots.

4 Brush the potatoes and shallots with oil and sprinkle with salt. Cook on the barbecue or grill (broil) for about 10 minutes, turning occasionally. Serve with the mustard dip.

Soaking the skewers

Bamboo skewers should be soaked in water for at least 20 minutes before threading on the vegetables. This will help prevent them burning during cooking.

Serves 4

INGREDIENTS
1kg/2¼lb small new potatoes, or
   larger potatoes halved
200g/7oz shallots, halved
30ml/2 tbsp olive oil
15ml/1 tbsp sea salt

For the mustard dip
4 garlic cloves, crushed
2 egg yolks
30ml/2 tbsp lemon juice
300ml/½ pint/1¼ cups extra virgin
   olive oil
10ml/2 tsp wholegrain mustard
salt and ground black pepper

This classic Greek snack, held together with a single spike, is perfect for serving with drinks as an informal appetizer. Teamed with wedges of watermelon, olives, salad and pitta bread, the parcels make a great lunch or supper.

sardine parcels with hot feta cheese dip

Serves 6

INGREDIENTS
12 fresh sardines
45ml/3 tbsp olive oil
2 shallots, finely chopped
3 garlic cloves, crushed
1 red chilli, seeded and
    finely chopped
small bunch coriander (cilantro) or
    flat leaf parsley, finely chopped
juice of 1 lemon
500g/1¼lb watermelon, cut into
    six wedges
warm pitta bread, Greek marinated
    olives and salad, to serve

For the dip
225g/8oz/1 cup Greek (US strained
    plain) yogurt
150ml/¼ pint/⅔ cup milk
450g/1lb feta cheese, crumbled
15ml/1 tbsp cornflour (cornstarch)
salt and ground black pepper

1 Soak 12 cocktail sticks (toothpicks) in water for about 30 minutes. Meanwhile, clean the sardines and remove the backbones. Heat 15ml/1 tbsp of the oil in a frying pan and add the shallots and garlic. Cook for a few minutes, then add the chilli and coriander or parsley.

2 Spread the shallot mixture over the flesh-side of the sardines, roll them up from the head to the tail and secure each one with a cocktail stick.

3 To make the dip, gently heat the yogurt and milk together until hot but not boiling, then add the cheese and stir until smooth. Blend the cornflour with 30ml/2 tbsp water and stir into the cheese mixture. Season to taste. Cook gently until thickened, then transfer to a heatproof bowl and place over a pan of gently simmering water to keep warm while you cook the sardines.

4 To cook the sardine parcels, heat the remaining olive oil in a frying pan and fry the sardines for 3–4 minutes. Add the lemon juice and transfer to a serving platter. Transfer the dip to a serving bowl, or a fondue set over a burner. Serve the sardine parcels with the watermelon wedges, warm pitta bread, olives and salad along with the hot dip.

grilled swordfish skewers

Skewered swordfish with peppers and onions is light and healthy, and perfect served with a summer salad after a hard day at work or for a light weekend lunch. Pop the skewers on the barbecue, then sit back and enjoy a glass of white wine while they cook.

Serves 4

INGREDIENTS
2 red onions, quartered
2 red or green (bell) peppers,
    quartered and seeded
20–24 thick cubes of swordfish,
    prepared weight 675g/1½lb
75ml/5 tbsp extra virgin olive oil
1 garlic clove, crushed
large pinch of dried oregano
salt and ground black pepper
tossed cucumber, onion and olive
    salad, to serve

1 Carefully separate the onion quarters in pieces, each composed of two or three layers. Slice each pepper quarter in half widthways.

2 Take four long metal skewers and thread five or six pieces of swordfish on to each one, alternating with pieces of pepper and onion. Set aside.

3 To make the basting sauce, put the olive oil, garlic and oregano in a bowl and whisk together. Season with salt and pepper and whisk again, then brush over the fish skewers generously on all sides.

4 Preheat the grill (broiler) to the highest setting or prepare a barbecue. Place the skewers under the grill or transfer to the barbecue, making sure that they are not too close to the heat. Cook for 8–10 minutes, turning and brushing with more basting sauce several times, until the fish is cooked and the peppers and onions have begun to scorch around the edges. Serve immediately with a tossed cucumber, onion and olive summer salad.

Preparing the swordfish
The fishmonger will prepare the cubes of swordfish for you, but if you prefer to do this yourself, you will need about 800g/1¾lb swordfish. Using a sharp knife, cut the fish into fairly large cubes – about 5cm/2in square.

These delicious bites are a contemporary version of Indonesian satay, and make a perfect appetizer or light meal. The sweet, spicy, tangy dipping sauce complements the marinated chicken perfectly.

honey-glazed chicken satay with spicy peanut sauce

1 Make the satay sauce by mixing the peanut butter, chilli, the juice of 1 lime and the coconut milk in a food processor or blender. Blend until smooth, then check the seasoning and add salt or more lime juice if necessary. Transfer the sauce to a bowl and set aside.

2 Slice each chicken breast portion into four long strips. To make the marinade, mix together the garlic, ginger, fish sauce, soy sauce and honey in a large bowl, then add the chicken strips and toss together until well coated. Cover the bowl with clear film (plastic wrap) and set aside for at least 30 minutes in the refrigerator. Meanwhile, soak 16 bamboo skewers in water, to prevent them from burning during cooking.

3 Preheat the grill (broiler) to high or prepare the barbecue. Drain the skewers. Drain the chicken strips and thread one strip on to each skewer. Grill (broil) for 3 minutes on each side, or until the chicken is golden brown and cooked through. Serve with the satay sauce.

Tasty alternatives
Try pork fillet (tenderloin) or large prawns (shrimp) instead of chicken – they are just as delicious when cooked on skewers and served with the spicy peanut sauce.

Serves 4

INGREDIENTS
4 skinless, boneless chicken
   breast portions

For the marinade
2 garlic cloves, crushed
2.5cm/1in piece fresh root
   ginger, grated
10ml/2 tsp Thai fish sauce
30ml/2 tbsp light soy sauce
15ml/1 tbsp clear honey

For the sauce
90ml/6 tbsp crunchy peanut butter
1 fresh red chilli, seeded and chopped
juice of 1–2 limes
60ml/4 tbsp coconut milk
salt

This simple recipe makes a substantial appetizer. Lemon grass stalks not only offer a decorative and unusual alternative to bamboo skewers, but also impart a wonderfully aromatic flavour.

griddled pork spiked on lemon grass sticks

Serves 4

INGREDIENTS
300g/11oz/2 cups minced (ground) pork
4 garlic cloves, crushed
4 fresh coriander (cilantro) roots,
    finely chopped
2.5ml/½ tsp granulated sugar
15ml/1 tbsp soy sauce
salt and ground black pepper
8 x 10cm/4in lengths of
    lemon grass stalk
sweet chilli sauce, to serve

1 Place the pork, garlic, chopped coriander root, sugar and soy sauce in a bowl. Season with salt and pepper and mix well until thoroughly combined. Divide the mixture into eight equal portions and, using your hands, mould each one into a ball.

2 Insert a length of lemon grass stalk halfway into each ball, then gently press the meat mixture around the lemon grass stalk to make a shape that resembles a chicken leg.

3 Cook the pork sticks under a hot grill (broiler) for 3–4 minutes on each side, until browned and cooked through. Serve immediately, offering the sweet chilli sauce as a dip.

Party snacks
This recipe can also be made into fabulous party snacks by pressing less pork mixture around each skewer. To make bitesize skewers, divide the pork mixture into 12 equal portions, then roll into balls and press around 12 lemon grass stalks. These smaller skewers will require a slightly shorter cooking time.

These pretty speared bundles use the Japanese cooking technique tataki, *which is used to cook rare steak. Chunks of beef are seared over a coal fire on long skewers, then plunged into cold water to stop the meat cooking further.*

speared beef wraps

Serves 4

INGREDIENTS
500g/1¼ lb chunk of beef thigh (a
    long, thin chunk looks better than
    a thick, round chunk)
generous pinch of salt
10ml/2 tsp vegetable oil

For the marinade
200ml/7fl oz/scant 1 cup rice vinegar
70ml/4½ tbsp sake
135ml/4½ fl oz/scant ⅔ cup shoyu
    (Japanese soy sauce)
15ml/1 tbsp caster (superfine) sugar
1 garlic clove, thinly sliced
1 small onion, thinly sliced
sansho (Japanese pepper)

To garnish
6 shiso (basil) leaves
½ salad cucumber
1 garlic clove, finely grated (optional)

1 Mix the marinade ingredients in a small pan and warm through until the sugar has dissolved. Remove from the heat and leave to cool.

2 Generously sprinkle the beef with the salt and rub into the meat. Leave to stand for 2–3 minutes, then rub in the oil evenly with your fingers.

3 Heat a griddle until very hot. Sear the beef, turning it frequently until about 5mm/¼ in of the flesh in from the surface is cooked. Immediately plunge the meat into a bowl of cold water for a few seconds. Wipe the meat with kitchen paper and immerse fully in the marinade. Chill for 1 day.

4 Next day, prepare the garnish. Chop the shiso leaves in half lengthways, then cut into very thin strips crossways. Slice the cucumber diagonally then cut the slices into matchsticks.

5 Remove the meat from the marinade. Strain the remaining marinade through a sieve, reserving both the liquid and the marinated onion and garlic. Using a sharp knife, cut the beef into slices about 5mm/¼ in thick.

6 Place the cucumber sticks and the marinated onion and garlic on the beef slices. Roll up and secure with cocktail sticks (toothpicks). Fluff the shiso strips and put on top of the beef. Serve with the reserved marinade in individual bowls and the grated garlic, if using.

sizeable skewers

Make a meal of it with fabulous skewered dishes. Tuck into chunky kebabs served with salad and pitta bread, enjoy fragrant rosemary skewers with a rich and creamy dolcelatte dipping sauce or try exotic delights such as spatchcock quail stuffed with spicy Moroccan-style couscous or stuffed squid.

Fonduta is the Italian version of fondue and is usually made from mixtures of Fontina, Provolone or Gorgonzola cheeses. For this recipe, creamy Dolcelatte cheese is mixed with mildly flavoured mozzarella.

rosemary skewers with Dolcelatte fonduta

Serves 4

INGREDIENTS

12 woody rosemary stems, about 15cm/
　6in long
12 slices prosciutto, sliced in half lengthways
400g/14oz walnut bread loaf, cut into
　large cubes
12 ready-to-eat prunes, pitted
2 courgettes (zucchini), halved lengthways
　and cut into 1cm/½in slices
25g/1oz/2 tbsp butter
30ml/2 tbsp olive oil
1 garlic clove, crushed

For the fonduta

450ml/¾ pint/scant 2 cups milk
200g/7oz Dolcelatte cheese, diced
115g/4oz/1 cup grated mozzarella cheese
15ml/1 tbsp cornflour (cornstarch)
60ml/4 tbsp dry white wine
salt and ground black pepper

1 Remove all but the top leaves from the rosemary stems and soak them in cold water for 30 minutes.

2 To make the fonduta, gently heat the milk in a fondue pot, then add the cheeses and stir until smooth. Season well. Blend the cornflour with the wine in a small bowl. Add to the cheese mixture and stir until thickened.

3 Meanwhile, prepare the rosemary skewers. Take a soaked rosemary stick and thread on one end of a slice of prosciutto. Add a bread cube, a prune and one or two slices of courgette, interleaving the prosciutto between the ingredients, so that the prosciutto slice is speared several times. Repeat with the other rosemary sticks.

4 Heat the butter with the oil in a large frying pan and gently fry the garlic for a few minutes. Add the skewers to the frying pan and cook for 1 minute on each side until hot and golden brown.

5 Place the fondue pot on a burner at the table. Diners can remove the vegetables from the skewers and use fondue forks to dip the vegetables into the hot Dolcelatte fonduta.

Serve these delicious, richly flavoured skewers with strips of chargrilled vegetables, which can be cooked on the barbecue alongside them. Accompany with a spicy dip and a stack of warm, soft pitta breads.

Moroccan fish brochettes with aromatic spices

Serves 6

INGREDIENTS
5 garlic cloves, chopped
2.5ml/½ tsp paprika
2.5ml/½ tsp ground cumin
2.5–5ml/½–1 tsp salt
2–3 pinches of cayenne pepper
60ml/4 tbsp olive oil
30ml/2 tbsp lemon juice
30ml/2 tbsp chopped fresh coriander (cilantro) or parsley
675g/1½ lb firm-fleshed white fish, such as haddock, halibut, sea bass, snapper or turbot, cut into 2.5–5cm/1–2in cubes
3–4 green (bell) peppers, cut into 2.5–5cm/1–2in pieces
2 lemon wedges, spicy dip and warm pitta bread, to serve

1 Put the garlic, paprika, cumin, salt, cayenne pepper, oil, lemon juice and coriander or parsley in a large bowl and mix together. Add the fish and toss to coat. Leave to marinate for at least 30 minutes, but preferably 2 hours at room temperature, or chill overnight.

2 About 40 minutes before you are going to cook the brochettes, light the barbecue. The barbecue is ready when the coals have turned white and grey.

3 Meanwhile, thread the fish cubes and pepper pieces alternately on to bamboo or metal skewers.

4 Grill the brochettes on the barbecue for 2–3 minutes on each side, or until the fish is tender and lightly browned. Serve with lemon wedges, a spicy dip and some warm pitta bread.

Using bamboo skewers
If you are using bamboo skewers for the brochettes, be sure to soak them in water for at least 20 minutes before using to prevent them from burning.

speared seafood cooked in miso-flavoured stock

This dish takes its inspiration from the traditional Mongolian firepot. Pretty pink prawn tails and cubes of fish are marinated with garlic, ginger and chilli, then skewered with fragrant lemon grass stalks before being cooked at the table in a rich stock.

1 Wash the prawns, pat dry and place in a deep serving bowl. Cut the salmon or tuna fillets into 2.5cm/1in cubes and add to the prawns.

2 Mix all the marinade ingredients together and add to the bowl of seafood. Toss gently to coat, then cover and leave the seafood to marinate in the refrigerator for a minimum of 10 minutes, or 2 hours if possible.

3 Pour the stock into a pan, add the coriander and spring onions and bring to the boil. Transfer to a fondue pot and place on a burner at the table or pour the stock into a firepot at the table and keep hot.

4 Arrange the salad leaves and mushrooms on serving plates, and put the soy sauce and wasabi or horseradish into small bowls. Add the noodles to the stock at the table and leave to cook.

5 Invite each diner to spear a cube of fish or a prawn on to a lemon grass stalk or bamboo skewer with a salad leaf and a mushroom. Submerge in the stock for 1 minute, or until the fish or prawn is cooked, then dip into the soy sauce and wasabi or horseradish. When the fish and vegetables are all eaten, divide the remaining stock and noodles among soup bowls to eat.

Easy-to-eat noodles
Snip the noodles into short lengths using a pair of kitchen scissors or just snap them using your hands to make them easier to eat at the table.

Serves 6

INGREDIENTS
8–12 whole king prawns (jumbo shrimp), peeled and deveined, with tails on
2 skinless salmon or tuna fillets, about 150g/5oz each
6 sachets instant miso soup mixed with 1.75 litres/3 pints/7½ cups water or the same quantity of fish, chicken or vegetable stock
handful of coriander (cilantro) leaves
2–3 spring onions (scallions), sliced
small bunch watercress, rocket (arugula) or young mizuna leaves
50g/2oz enoki mushrooms
200g/7oz fine egg noodles
8–12 lemon grass stalks or bamboo skewers
soy sauce and wasabi paste or horseradish sauce, to serve

For the marinade
rind and juice of 2 limes
15ml/1 tbsp soy sauce
2.5cm/1in piece fresh root ginger, peeled and finely chopped
2 garlic cloves, finely chopped
15ml/1 tbsp clear honey
1 red chilli, seeded and chopped

These Thai-style stuffed squid are held together with a small spike and cooked in a delicious, aromatic coconut milk sauce. They are perfect served with a simple bowl of plain boiled rice.

spiked Thai stuffed squid

1 Clean the squid, leaving them whole. Set aside with the tentacles. To make the stuffing, put the white fish, ginger and spring onions in a large mortar. Add a little salt and pound to a paste with a pestle. Use a food processor, if you prefer.

2 Transfer the fish paste to a bowl and stir in the prawns. Using a spoon or a piping bag, fill the squid with the stuffing. Tuck the tentacles inside the squid and secure the top of each one with a cocktail stick (toothpick).

3 To make the sauce, put the nuts and galangal in a food processor. Remove the lower 5cm/2in from the lemon grass stalks and put aside. Chop the remaining stem roughly and add to the processor with the shrimp paste, chillies and onions. Process to a paste.

4 Heat the oil in a wok and fry the mixture. Using a rolling pin, bruise the remaining lemon grass and add to the wok with the coconut milk. Stir constantly until the sauce boils, then lower the heat and simmer for about 5 minutes.

5 Arrange the squid in the sauce, and cook for 15–20 minutes. Taste and season with salt and lime juice, if using. Serve with boiled rice.

Preparing squid

Cleaned squid is readily available, which is a definite bonus. Wash thoroughly inside the pocket to make sure that all the quill has been removed.

Serves 2

INGREDIENTS

8 small squid, each about 10cm/4in
    long, total weight about 350g/12oz
lime juice (optional)
salt

For the stuffing

175g/6oz white fish fillets, skinned
2.5cm/1in piece fresh root ginger,
    peeled and finely sliced
2 spring onions (scallions), chopped
salt
50g/2oz peeled cooked prawns
    (shrimp), roughly chopped

For the sauce

4 macadamia nuts or almonds
1cm/½in piece fresh galangal, peeled
2 lemon grass stalks, root trimmed
1cm/½in cube shrimp paste
4 fresh red chillies, seeded and
    roughly chopped
175g/6oz small onions, roughly chopped
60–90ml/4–6 tbsp vegetable oil
400ml/14fl oz can coconut milk

stuffed spatchcock quail

These delicate game birds can be pressed flat and skewered to keep them in position while they are cooked over a barbecue with a lid. Serve with a salad of halved cherry tomatoes soaked in olive oil, seasoned and sprinkled with plenty of fresh basil.

Serves 8

INGREDIENTS
8 quail
400ml/14fl oz/1⅔ cups water
2 lemons
60ml/4 tbsp extra virgin olive oil
45ml/3 tbsp fresh tarragon leaves
115g/4oz/generous ⅔ cup couscous
15g/½oz dried (bell) peppers,
   finely chopped
8 black olives, pitted and chopped
salt and ground black pepper

1 Cut the backbones away from each quail and place them in a pan. Add the water and bring to the boil, then simmer gently until reduced by half. Meanwhile, wipe the insides of each bird with kitchen paper. Place each quail in turn, breast uppermost, on a board, and flatten by pressing firmly on the breastbone. Carefully loosen the quail skin over the breasts.

2 Grate the rind from the lemons. Set half the rind aside and put the rest in a flat dish. Squeeze both lemons into the dish and add 30ml/2 tbsp of the oil and 15ml/1 tbsp of the tarragon. Add the quail, turn to coat and leave to marinate.

3 Place the couscous in a bowl and add the dried peppers and seasoning. Strain 200ml/7fl oz/scant 1 cup of the reduced quail stock over the couscous. Leave to stand for about 10 minutes.

4 Mix in the reserved lemon rind with the olives and the remaining tarragon and oil. Spread the mixture on a plate to cool, then cover and chill. When cold, ease a little stuffing into the breast pocket on each quail. You will need 16 skewers. If using bamboo ones, soak them in water for 20 minutes.

5 Prepare the barbecue. Pin the legs and wings of each quail to the body by driving a long skewer through either side, forming a cross.

6 Place the spatchcocked quail on a lightly oiled rack over the barbecue and cook for about 5 minutes, moving the birds around occasionally. Cover with a lid or tented heavy-duty foil and cook for 10 minutes, or until the birds are plump and nicely browned. Leave to stand for a few minutes before serving.

These richly flavoured kebabs are fabulous served inside warm pitta bread filled with fresh crunchy vegetable salad and drizzled with creamy, nutty tahini.

Jerusalem-style lamb kebabs

Serves 4–6

INGREDIENTS
800g/1¾ lb tender lamb, cubed
1.5ml/¼ tsp ground allspice
1.5ml/¼ tsp ground cinnamon
1.5ml/¼ tsp ground black pepper
1.5ml/¼ tsp ground cardamom
45–60ml/3–4 tbsp chopped
   fresh parsley
2 onions, chopped
5–8 garlic cloves, chopped
juice of ½ lemon or 45ml/3 tbsp dry
   white wine
45ml/3 tbsp extra virgin olive oil
sumac, for sprinkling (optional)
30ml/2 tbsp pine nuts
salt
warm pitta bread, tahini and vegetable
   salad, to serve

1 Put the lamb, allspice, cinnamon, black pepper, cardamom, half the parsley, half the onions, the garlic, lemon juice or wine and olive oil in a bowl and mix together. Season with salt or, if you prefer, sprinkle on the salt after cooking. Set aside and leave to marinate.

2 Meanwhile, light the barbecue and leave for about 40 minutes. When the coals are white and grey, the barbecue is ready. If using bamboo skewers, soak them in water for about 20 minutes to prevent them from burning.

3 Thread the cubes of meat on to bamboo or metal skewers, then cook on the barbecue for 2–3 minutes on each side, turning them occasionally, until cooked evenly and browned.

4 Transfer the kebabs to a serving dish and sprinkle with the reserved onions, parsley, sumac, if using, pine nuts and salt, if you like. Serve with warm pitta breads to wrap the kebabs in, a bowl of tahini for drizzling over and a vegetable salad.

Using sumac
Sumac is a Middle-Eastern spice and is definitely worth buying if it is available. Its tangy flavour is fresh and invigorating, and its red colour is appealing.

dessert on a stick

Skewered fruit, meringues, marshmallows and other confectionery make interesting and unusual desserts. Grilling sweet skewers or spiking desserts on sticks, then dipping them into a luscious sauce are all fabulous ways to end a meal.

Grilled fruits make a perfect end to a meal and look very pretty cut into bitesize chunks and threaded on to skewers. The lemon grass sticks used here give the fruit a subtle fragrant flavour.

exotic fruit skewers with tangy lime cheese

1 Prepare the barbecue or preheat the grill (broiler). Using a sharp knife, cut the top of each lemon grass stalk into a point. Remove the outer leaves from the stalk and discard, then use the back of the knife to lightly bruise the length of each stalk to release the aromatic oils. Thread each stalk with a few of the fruit pieces and bay leaves.

2 Support a piece of foil on a baking sheet and roll up the edges to make a rim. Grease the foil, lay the kebabs on top and grate a little nutmeg over them. Drizzle the maple syrup over and dust liberally with the demerara sugar. Grill (broil) for about 5 minutes, until the fruit is lightly charred.

3 Meanwhile, make the lime cheese. Put the cheese, cream, grated lime rind and juice and icing sugar in a bowl and mix together until thoroughly combined. Serve immediately with the fruit kebabs.

Using lemon grass

When choosing lemon grass stalks to use as skewers, always look for fresh ones. Bottled lemon grass stalks are widely available and have a good flavour but they are too soft to use for skewering foods.

Serves 4

INGREDIENTS

4 long, fresh lemon grass stalks
1 mango, peeled, stoned (pitted) and
    cut into chunks
1 papaya, peeled, seeded and cut
    into chunks
1 star fruit, cut into thick slices
    and halved
8 fresh bay leaves
1 nutmeg
60ml/4 tbsp maple syrup
50g/2oz/¼ cup demerara (raw) sugar

For the lime cheese

150g/5oz/⅔ cup curd cheese or
    low-fat soft cheese
120ml/4fl oz/½ cup double
    (heavy) cream
grated rind and juice of ½ lime
30ml/2 tbsp icing (confectioners') sugar

Spiral-shaped marzipan pastries and sweet fresh figs are wonderful skewered on long-handled forks, then dipped into a piping hot blackberry-and-wine dipping sauce. It is a perfect dessert during the blackberry season.

speared figs and pastries with hot blackberry sauce

Serves 4–6

INGREDIENTS
16 ripe, fresh figs, quartered

For the pastries
plain (all-purpose) flour and icing (confectioners') sugar, for dusting and rolling
375g/13oz puff pastry, thawed if frozen
275g/10oz white marzipan
caster (superfine) sugar, for dusting

For the sauce
800g/1¾lb/7 cups blackberries
juice of 2 lemons
175g/6oz/scant 1 cup caster (superfine) sugar
300ml/½ pint/1¼ cups rosé wine
30ml/2 tbsp cornflour (cornstarch) blended to a paste with about 30ml/2 tbsp water
105ml/7 tbsp crème de cassis
15ml/1 tbsp chopped fresh mint

1 To make the pastries, preheat the oven to 180°C/350°F/Gas 4, line a baking sheet with baking parchment, and dust a work surface with flour. Roll out the pastry to a 30 x 20cm/12 x 8in rectangle, then dust the work surface with icing sugar and roll out the marzipan to the same size.

2 Place the marzipan on top of the pastry, then roll up both together to make a long sausage shape. Cut crossways into 1cm/½in slices using a large, sharp knife and arrange on the prepared baking sheet. Bake for 15 minutes, or until puffed and tinged golden brown. Transfer to a wire rack, and dust with caster sugar.

3 To make the sauce, blend the blackberries in a food processor with the lemon juice, then press through a sieve into a pan. Add the sugar and wine and bring to the boil, then simmer for about 20 minutes, skimming off any scum that rises to the top. Stir in the blended cornflour and cook, stirring, until thickened. Stir in the crème de cassis.

4 Transfer the sauce to a fondue pot, add the mint, and place on a burner at the table. Spear the figs on fondue forks and serve with the pastries and the hot dipping sauce.

spiked fruity meringues with crème anglaise

Dainty meringues filled with raspberry purée and served with fresh berries are fabulous speared on decorative skewers and dipped into a creamy vanilla custard. If you have a fondue set, use it to keep the sauce warm at the table.

Serves 4–6

INGREDIENTS
115g/4oz/⅔ cup fresh raspberries
3 egg whites
175g/6oz/scant 1 cup caster
    (superfine) sugar
200g/7oz/1¾ cups fresh summer
    berries, to serve

For the crème anglaise
120ml/4fl oz/½ cup milk
300ml/½ pint/1¼ cups single
    (light) cream
1 vanilla pod (bean), split lengthways
1 fresh bay leaf
4 egg yolks
50g/2oz/¼ cup vanilla-flavoured caster
    (superfine) sugar

1 Preheat the oven to 120°C/250°F/Gas ½ and line two baking trays with baking parchment.

2 To make the meringues, first purée the raspberries in a food processor or blender, then strain through a sieve. Whisk the egg whites until they hold stiff peaks. Add the sugar, a tablespoonful at a time, whisking between each addition until you have a light, firm and glossy meringue.

3 Place small heaps of the meringue mixture (about two teaspoonfuls) well apart on the baking trays, and make a slight hollow in the centre of each with the back of a wet teaspoon. Place a teaspoonful of the raspberry purée into each hollow, then top with a little more meringue. Bake for 1½ hours, or until crisp but slightly soft in the centre.

4 To make the crème anglaise, heat the milk and cream in a pan with the vanilla pod and bay leaf until almost boiling. Whisk the egg yolks and sugar together until pale and creamy, then whisk in the hot cream mixture. Return to a very low heat and stir constantly until thickened.

5 Transfer the custard to a warmed serving bowl, and serve with the raspberry meringues and berries for dipping.

sweet and sticky strawberry and marshmallow kebabs

After cooking, dredge these little kebabs with plenty of icing sugar, some of which will soak into the strawberry juice. To produce pretty grill marks, the grill should be very hot to sear the marshmallows quickly before they have time to melt. The dark cherry wood skewers contrast very prettily with the pale marshmallows and red strawberries.

1 Prepare the barbecue. If you are using cherry wood skewers, soak them in water for at least 30 minutes.

2 When the coals are hot or with a light coating of ash, lightly oil the grill rack and position it just above the coals to heat.

3 Wash and hull the strawberries, then spike two marshmallows and two strawberries on each drained wooden or metal skewer and grill over the hot coals for about 20 seconds on each side. If grill marks don't appear quickly, don't persist for too long: cook only until the marshmallows are warm and just beginning to melt.

4 Transfer the strawberry and marshmallow kebabs to individual dessert plates or a large platter, dust generously with icing sugar and serve immediately.

If you can't find cherry wood spikes
Plain bamboo skewers that have been soaked in water for at least 20 minutes make a good substitute if you can't get hold of cherry wood sticks. You can also use metal skewers, although you should be careful when handling them because they heat up through their whole length very quicky.

Serves 4

INGREDIENTS
8 short lengths of cherry
 wood for skewers (optional)
16 strawberries
16 marshmallows
icing (confectioners') sugar,
 for dusting

These delightful treats are always a hit with kids. They can be decorated with a variety of colourful candies or in a slightly more grown-up way with additional chocolate decorations.

chocolate cookie crumble on a stick

Makes 12

INGREDIENTS
125g/4¼oz milk chocolate
75g/3oz white chocolate
50g/2oz plain (semisweet)
   chocolate biscuits (cookies),
   crumbled into chunks
12 wooden ice lolly (popsicle) sticks
selection of small coloured sweets
   (candies), chocolate chips or
   chocolate-coated raisins

1 Break the milk and white chocolate into separate heatproof bowls and melt first the milk chocolate, then the white over a pan of gently simmering water, stirring frequently until smooth.

2 Meanwhile, draw six 7cm/2¾in rounds on a sheet of baking parchment and six 9 x 7cm/3½ x 2¾in rectangles. Invert the paper on to a large tray.

3 Spoon the milk chocolate mixture into the marked shapes and spread to the edges with the back of a teaspoon. Gently press the end of an ice lolly stick into each. Before the chocolate has time to set, sprinkle liberally with the crumbled chocolate biscuits.

4 Using a teaspoon, drizzle thin lines of the melted white chocolate back and forth over the lollies so that the crumbled biscuits and milk chocolate show through in places.

5 Very gently, press sweets, chocolate chips or chocolate-coated raisins into the melted chocolate. Chill for about 1 hour until set, then carefully peel away the paper.

index